MW01032374

GLOBAL
ADVENTURES
IN SHORT-TERM MISSIONS

A PRACTICAL GUIDE FOR
360° SPIRITUAL DEVELOPMENT

Presented by:

Enduring Treasure
Ministries, Inc.

Copyright © 2015 by Enduring Treasure Ministries, Inc.

www.enduringtreasureministries.org

All rights reserved. No part of this publication may be reproduced, distributed, or transmitted in any form or by any means, including photocopying, recording, or other electronic or mechanical methods, without the prior written permission of the publisher, except in the case of brief quotations embodied in critical reviews and certain other noncommercial uses permitted by copyright law.

Printed in the United States of America

First Edition

ISBN-13: 978-1511931601
ISBN-10: 1511931604

BISAC: Religion / Christian Ministry / Missions

Acknowledgements

A well-rounded philosophy of short-term ministry is something that is developed over years of experience and through interaction with many individuals. It is impossible to mention everyone or to track down the source of every idea presented. It is necessary, though, to recognize that there have been many contributors to this resource.

Certainly, our greatest teachers have been our international ministry partners who have contributed so much to our development and growth. It is our privilege to acknowledge the vital role they have played in placing this resource the hands of God's people.

Many of the materials found in this book were developed during the time of our service with the team at Every Generation Ministries. We wish to acknowledge EGM's part in the launching of Enduring Treasure Ministries and thank the staff for their part in shaping our short-term ministry beliefs and practices.

We also want to thank Calvary Church of Saint Peters, Missouri for contributions to the appendix section of this resource and recognize Jerry Montante, Jeannette Cox and Barbara Guthmiller for help with editing.

We're trusting God to bless each of you, as your part in the development of this book results in 360° spiritual impact around the world.

CONTENTS

Introduction

So, you're ready for a new adventure. Great! This adventure you're taking will make a lasting impression on everyone connected. It's a 360° impact. Donors, prayer partners, ministry leaders, those you serve and you—all can experience God at work through this short-term mission. You'll want to be well prepared.

Going on one of these adventures is a little bit like jumping in a car while it's speeding down the road because you're jumping into the middle of what God has already been doing. The national or mission partner that you're joining has been there for months, years or even decades, faithfully serving God. Your contribution is valuable but is not necessarily the start of God's Kingdom work.

Don't get the wrong idea. Your ministry is significant and if done in the power of God will leave its mark for all eternity! But it is HIS work that lasts, not ours. God doesn't need someone from another culture to go on a short-term mission trip to change the world. He's already doing it! The thrill is that He invites you to join Him and share in the joy of serving others.

Another way this trip is like jumping into that speeding car is that it's wild and crazy and a little bit frightening. On the other hand it is exhilarating to join God in the work that He is doing. One thing for sure...you will never be the same. When God calls you to make a bold move, like going on a short-term mission, He has your best interest in mind as well. He has things to show you and teach you.

This guide has been written to help you as you make that grand leap. It offers some practical tips on being prepared to enter a different culture. Being aware of the details and variances enables you to get on board for your message to be heard.

The spiritual training portion will prepare your heart for that jump. It takes someone strong in the Lord to make a bold move. Short-term trips require that we not be easily overwhelmed by strange foods, uncomfortable beds or crowded buses. A spiritually strong person will look at each of those challenges as just one more way God is doing His work of changing us.

When the time comes for you to jump off that speeding car of an adventure and return home, the work that God has planned for that field will continue moving down that road. God will still be lovingly reaching the people you have served. He will continue to encourage and strengthen His servants on the mission field. And long after you unpack your suitcase, He will still be working in YOUR life to shape you into the person He desires you to be.

So, go! Enjoy the journey and hold on to your hat. It's going to be the trip of a lifetime!

SHORT-TERM MISSION TRIP BASICS

A PHILOSOPHY FOR SHORT-TERM MISSIONS

If you are reading this guidebook, it shows you have a heart to further God's Kingdom around the globe and have a desire to learn more about all that it requires. That's exciting!

Many organizations and churches offer mission trips as an "adventure" or a "vacation with a purpose." Traveling does enrich your life and expand your worldview. However, mission trips can be much more.

If you carefully examine your motives, properly adjust your perspective and plan prayerfully, it's possible that your involvement on this mission trip could be the key to completing important ministry work on your chosen field. This trip will certainly leave an enduring mark on you and will hopefully have a lasting impression on those to whom you minister.

As a team member you must work alongside your church or ministry staff to gain their valuable insights. In preparation for your international adventure, it's recommended that you first have an adventure in God's Word. If you do this, the process of preparing for your trip may change your perception of God's Kingdom work and how you can be involved.

Each individual is unique and has a specific role to play, enabling the team to be effective. Working together as a team will allow additional opportunities to learn from and strengthen each other. We know that each person participating in a mission trip will bring with them a wide variety of ministry styles and experience. Together we are able to achieve so much more.

We pray that your visit will be a special blessing to international partners as well. Providing encouragement to Christian leaders is a key purpose in arranging mission trips. Whether you are laying flooring in an office, coaching a pastor, speaking at a seminar for children's workers or helping with crafts at a camp, your smile and helping hands can be a great blessing. The investment that each team member makes through personal involvement increases the effectiveness of those we serve and continues to impact their ministry long after the team returns home.

We believe that your visit will enrich your spiritual journey as well and that you will return home encouraged and challenged. A short-term ministry trip has potential to leave its imprint for years to come, on everyone who is involved.

TYPES OF SHORT-TERM MISSION TRIPS

There are many types of ministry trips that enable churches and ministries to support global partners. Following are several of the most common types of short-term mission trips.

OUTREACH SUPPORT TRIPS

During an outreach trip, short-term teams can provide needed support to national teams as they seek to reach out to the unreached in their communities. Foreign involvement can, in some cultures, pique interest and participation in outreach events. Personal evangelism efforts can sometimes be more effective when outsiders participate.

MEDICAL SUPPORT TRIPS

In many parts of the world, access to medical resources is limited. In these places, a medical team coming from outside the culture can be a big benefit to national Christians seeking to serve their communities. Medical teams can be involved in general medical assistance, can provide dental services, assess and treat vision challenges, etc. In addition to providing medical services, these teams can express the love of Christ in tangible ways and can also help non-believers to be receptive to the communication of the life-changing Gospel of Jesus Christ.

TRAINING SUPPORT TRIPS

Training teams can be small. They are sometimes even made up of three people or less. Teams of experienced ministry leaders can make a huge difference in the ongoing ministry of national workers by sharing at specialized training events. Training trip teams can present an almost unlimited number of training topics: leadership topics, age-group related subject materials (such as a children's ministry training or youth training), and more. Providing creative resources is a key part of developing effective ministry leaders among the national workers and assisting them in conducting effective ministry programs in their local churches. It's important to note that we often learn as much (or more) from our national ministry partners as we teach.

PROGRAM SUPPORT TRIPS

You may be invited to participate with ministry partners that require additional help with a variety of projects. Program support teams might assist with office renovations, planning and preparing for a leadership development conference or serving in some type of children's ministry. These mission trips provide a great opportunity to work alongside national Christian workers and share in the joys of serving the Lord through serving others.

The relationships formed provide ongoing benefits for years to come.

VISION/RESEARCH TRIPS

Church and ministry leadership occasionally arrange a trip to explore new ministry opportunities, evaluate ongoing ministry progress or to provide for a hands-on experience for ministry supporters. It is vital for key leadership and donors to experience the field needs first hand in order for them to develop and implement effective strategies for ministry.

All of these types of trips are used by God to bring His treasured Word to His treasured people. By considering different approaches and working together, teams can effectively utilize their God-given gifts to support the work God is already doing on the fields where He calls us to serve.

BEFORE
THE TRIP

What needs to be done before your trip?

SPIRITUAL PREPARATION

Often, short-term ministry team members focus most of their pre-trip preparation on the physical side of things. While physical preparations are important, it is most important to remember to prepare yourself to serve by preparing your heart.

Setting aside time to spend with God should continue throughout the entire ministry process—while you are preparing, while you are on the field and when you return as part of your normal Christian walk.

Serving and *flexibility* are key words in ministry. It is often difficult to lay aside our ideas for what we think should be done in order to serve and meet the needs of others, but that is what we must do to have an effective ministry. It is the preparation that you do spiritually that will enable you to minister effectively with the heart of a servant, willing to be flexible according to the needs of others as God directs you by His Spirit.

Effective practical ministry is the result of dedicated spiritual preparation—your time alone with God.

Spiritual preparation should include prayer, spending time in the Word and even journaling.

Spend time in prayer. Spend concentrated time each day praying for God's direction for you as you prepare for your part of the ministry trip. Pray for opportunities to encourage your team members. Begin now to pray for the national workers you will be meeting during your trip and those that will be impacted by the team's ministry.

Spend time reading God's Word. Reading God's Word and studying some key passages will also be beneficial. Choosing a few passages to memorize will be valuable for your personal growth and encouragement during your trip. It will allow you to meditate on His Word even when you are busy with other activities.

There is a team devotional Bible study guide located in the Appendix of this book which will help you to prepare spiritually as a team.

Keep a personal journal. Keeping a personal journal is a great way to record all the things God is teaching you as you prepare and make this trip. In your journal you can record meaningful passages of Scripture, prayers, experiences—good, bad and indifferent, things you are learning, notes about the relationships you are forming, etc. This written document will become a life-long record of God's faithfulness in preparing you and using you to serve others.

There are journal pages for your use in the Appendix section of this book.

PHYSICAL PREPARATION

The physical preparations necessary will depend on the type of ministry trip that you are involved with. Team members with health issues can enjoy fruitful ministry experiences. However, being in good health will certainly help you to view your trip from a more positive perspective and will make it easier for you. Be sure to discuss the specific physical demands of your particular trip with your team leader. Be honest about your limitations. If you have any health concerns it is always wise to check with your doctor before traveling.

Increase your stamina. One thing that will make any ministry trip easier is getting your body ready for lots of walking. Transportation is often limited and may require your team to walk more than you are accustomed to here in the U.S. If you are not used to walking long distances, you may want to begin to condition your body for this before you travel.

Get your shots. Some of the locations where mission trips take place will require special shots. Specific recommendations of medical professionals concerning the country being visited should be communicated to the team. We recommend that you get a tetanus booster if you have not had one in the past five years.

Be prepared for accidents. Most trips are completed without incident. However, accidents do happen and medical needs do surface at times during short-term mission trips. Precautions taken before departure may be more crucial than you think.

Get advice from the field. Your church or ministry is in contact with individuals on the chosen field of ministry. They will have specific information about what to expect and will be able to make some good recommendations for how you need to physically prepare for your short-term ministry experience.

TECHNICAL TRAINING AND PLANNING

Because every trip is unique, the technical training and planning is different for each. Your team leader will help you find a role on the trip where you can contribute your gifts and abilities to ministry trip objectives. Team leaders make the final appointments of duties and set deadlines for projects. The amount of time spent on this portion of your preparation will depend on the type of ministry project with which you are going to be involved.

In some cases, team members may be asked to provide written materials used in training programs. Plan well in advance of your trip regarding any translation of materials that may be needed in order for your ministry to be of value to those who speak another language.

National ministry partners will usually do their best to provide an excellent job of getting materials translated but can only do so if they receive the information in a timely fashion. Communicate with your field hosts to understand how translation can be handled and paid for.

FINANCIAL AND PRAYER SUPPORT

It is the responsibility of the team leader to create a trip budget. Trip budgets include things like: airfare, accommodations, food, transport (on the field), visa costs, ministry expenses, travel insurance, and more. Budgets may also include an administration fee that covers the costs of coordinating the trip and managing the administrative details.

The needed support for the ministry of each missionary is provided by God through individuals and churches. This support comes in the form of both prayer and financial contributions. As a short-term missionary you will want to share your ministry needs with others.

Your network of prayer supporters and your network of financial supporters will overlap. This network generally includes family, friends and acquaintances as well as your local church. Think carefully through the relationships you have. As you do this, you should be able to begin to create a list of potential ministry partners. This list can serve as both a mailing list and a prayer list. Ongoing communication with these partners will benefit you and your ministry and may even lead to connecting these partners with the ministry on the field long term.

Prayer Support Discovery

Develop a prayer network. Once you have decided that God has called you to join a mission trip team, your top priority should be given to forming a prayer network to pray with you throughout your adventure in short-term ministry. These individuals and their commitment to pray will be a significant part of your overall ministry experience and effectiveness. They will be silent partners on the team.

There is a Potential Ministry Partners worksheet located in the

Appendix section of this book which can help you develop your prayer partner list.

Spend time praying as a team. Each time you meet, your team will spend time in prayer together. However, you will also want to share your ministry opportunity with others that will be praying for you now and throughout the trip. Gathering small groups together for prayer and encouraging individuals to pray will provide you with great support.

Besides your own personal needs you can share requests for your team like the details in the preparation process, needed finances to cover the trip expenses and the unity of the group. Include prayer points for the international team that you are joining. Pray for good communication and understanding of the cultural differences on both sides. Pray that others would be drawn to the Lord and their lives impacted by your team's ministry.

Financial Support Discovery

While prayer partners are crucial to the support of the spiritual side of the ministry, financial partners are also needed for the physical aspects of the work being done.

Certain biblical principles serve as the basis for Christian ministers raising financial support in order to meet their material needs.

- God calls His servants into ministry and those who are called are worthy of support. (1 Timothy 4:17-18, 1 Corinthians 9:1-18)

- It is appropriate for missionaries to provide information regarding their needs. (1 Corinthians 9:4-5)

- The advancement of the Gospel always takes precedence

over the needs of the missionary. (1 Corinthians 9:15-16, 2 Thessalonians 3:9)

- Those whom God has called are to build partnerships with those who support their ministry. (Philippians 1:3-5, 4:14-18)

- God is able to meet all of our needs. (Philippians 4:19)

Communicate your vision. The first step in the support discovery process is being able to communicate your ministry vision and purpose. You will need to understand your team's purpose and your individual purpose for this trip. You will need to be able to share how God has called you and prepared you. You will need to tell about the long term results of your ministry trip. These are the things that draw others into desiring to join you by praying and giving. You can communicate through personal interactions, group meetings or even letters. Your team leader will have more detailed suggestions for your team.

Build relationships. As you discover your list of financial supporters you will also be building relationships with them. They will want to be involved in your life and ministry in order to better pray for you and to evaluate the effectiveness of their financial giving. You will want to reciprocate by reaching out to them throughout your time of preparation and during the ministry trip.

Communicate frequently and creatively. Phone calls, letters and emails are critical for maintaining good communication. Social media can be used quite effectively as you seek to keep your support team updated. This may or may not work during your travels depending on location. You will definitely want to report back to each one when you return so they can praise God with you for the work He has done in and through you.

For more resources on support discovery see the Appendix section of this book.

CULTURAL PREPARATION

Culture is a reality. So is culture shock! By doing some homework before you arrive you can avoid some of the discomfort that comes from being immersed into a culture different than your own.

Take a close look at your own culture. Take time to know yourself and what makes you tick. Think about the culture that you are familiar with in your church, your community and in the United States. Ask yourself how your team may be viewed by those outside of the group. Would you be seen as spiritual, judgmental, loud, opinionated, servant-hearted, rich, wise, etc.?

Explore the culture of the place you will be visiting. Investigate their history. Discover some of their customs. What are some common foods and drinks? How does the average person dress? How is Christianity viewed in this culture?

Seek to familiarize yourself with the language. It will probably not be necessary for you to be fluent in the language of your target field. However, knowing just a few phrases will show them you value their culture. Even if those words are not pronounced perfectly it honors your hosts when you take the time to learn how to say things like, "Thank you," "Please," etc.

You may want to check out these websites for cultural and country information:

> www.operationworld.org
> www.odci.gov/cia/publications/pub.html
> www.expateexchange.com

The book *Foreign to Familiar* by Sarah A. Lanier is an interesting look into the cross-cultural experience. The short chapters make it an easy read and the ideas presented will be extremely beneficial to creating a positive environment for ministry to take place. Although there are many other books that discuss the cross-culturaldifferences, this is the one that should be required reading.

Your team leader should have more information provided by your international ministry partners that will help you to be a little more prepared when you arrive.

DURING
THE TRIP

What will you experience during your trip?

SPIRITUAL STRENGTHENING

Maintaining a spiritual focus will be crucial to achieving the goals of your mission trip. It will be critical for you to spend time in the Word and in prayer *each* day. This can be a real challenge when you are on a mission trip. However, your schedule should include time for personal devotion and reflection (journaling) as well as time with the team to worship and study each day. Your team leader will give you further instructions that will help you in this area.

There is a Bible study guide for on-the-field team devotional study in the Appendix section of this book.

PHYSICAL EXPECTATIONS

Connect on arrival. Most teams arrive on the field weary from travel, but still excited and ready to begin. In most cases, you will be met upon arrival by a national representative who will guide you to your accommodations and help you get settled so you can freshen up and have a brief rest. It's best not to jump immediately into ministry. Rather, your first day on the field should include time to unwind and adjust to your new surroundings, including the new time zone.

Be flexible about accommodations. Accommodations vary dramatically from country to country and will depend on what type of ministry you are involved with. Remember to be flexible.

It can be challenging, at times, to rest well in unfamiliar surroundings. Beds, pillows and bedding may be very different from what you are used to at home. It is important to appreciate the efforts made by your hosts to make you comfortable. Many hosts sacrifice much in order to provide what is perceived as the needs of American visitors.

Give new foods a chance. Meal time may also be a time of adjustment. Your host country may be on a very different meal schedule, the foods may look and taste unusual from your normal meals or you might see common foods eaten in a new way. Think ketchup on your pizza or soup for breakfast or eating dinner at midnight. Be willing to give new things a chance and you might be pleasantly surprised! Suggestions concerning eating have more to do with courtesy than with caution, though care is always necessary.

Be a gracious guest. You may have opportunity to eat with a family in their home while you are on the trip. Most will offer you the very best they have and will serve you before they serve themselves. Be both honored and humbled by their offerings of love and hospitality, even if you do not particularly care for what is set before you.

Thankfulness is most appreciated when expressed simply and sincerely.

Embrace local foods. If you are eating in restaurants your host will be able to help you determine what is on the menu so that you can order something you will enjoy. You may see a restaurant chain that you recognize from home. Although a bit of the familiar is always nice when travelling, it will be important for you to experience the culture where you serve and that experience will include the foods of your hosting culture. Be sensitive about requesting a trip to one of your favorite fast food restaurants. These are often very expensive compared to other restaurants in the area. It's best to allow your host to make arrangements for you to simply participate appreciatively.

Be prepared for unfamiliar restroom situations. Restroom accommodations also vary drastically from one area to another. It is wise to carry your own tissues at all times. Toilets and showers may be different from what you are used to or comfortable with. Your team leader will have information about what you can expect and how you should prepare.

Be sensitive with bathroom use. Before using the restroom or shower in someone's home, it's always wise to ask your host if there are any special instructions. When it is time to get ready in the morning be sure to keep it simple. Reduce shower time to save on hot water. Remember that you are only one in a group of people that may need a shower. There is only one bathroom for several people so be considerate of others. Hair dryers and other similar items can sometimes be cause for electricity problems. If at all possible, plan to do without these luxuries while travelling.

Travel the way the locals do. Be prepared to do lots of walking. The use of public transportation is often a part of a short-term ministry trip. If your host arranges for private transportation, be prepared to experience a different driving experience from what you are used to. Observations about the differences may or may not be welcome. If you have concerns about your transportation, it's best to communicate them through your team leader and not directly to your hosts or drivers.

There is a Release of Rights form in the Appendix section of this book that can be used to think through the various challenges you might face and systematically give those to God.

TECHNICAL TRAINING AND PLANNING

Meet your national team hosts. Once you arrive in the host country your team leader should arrange a time for your team to meet the national team that you will be serving with while you are visiting. This will be the foundation for a great time of ministry and fellowship. During this initial meeting you will probably receive an updated schedule for your time on the field. There may or may not be changes from what was previously given so maintain that flexible spirit and be open to what God has in store.

Be respectful. As you meet with your newest team members keep in mind that they have been preparing as well and have ideas that will be valuable to the success of the ministry. Because they know the language, culture, and perhaps the individuals you will be serving, they will have a good understanding of what methods and activities will be most effective. Be respectful of their ideas. Listen with an open mind and heart.

Follow good communication practices. While on location, your questions and concerns should continue to be directed to your team leader. Your team leader will, in turn, be the one responsible to communicate the needs of the team to the national representative. Working through these channels of leadership should eliminate most communication problems.

FINANCIAL AND PRAYER SUPPORTERS

Remember your sending team. Even though you are miles from home, your prayer partners and financial supporters will be with you each step of the way. They will be praying for you and your team and the ministry you're involved with. In return, you can be praying for them. Ask God to show you things to share with them when you return so that they can see the value of their contribution to your ministry.

Record your thoughts and impressions. It is good to keep these people in mind as you jot down stories and quotes in your journal, take pictures, find interesting souvenirs from the country where you are serving, etc. While you are in the midst of ministry, plan what you want to share and ways to do that with these important partners in your ministry.

Update your sending team in real time if possible. With the technology available today it can be much easier to keep those at home informed and up to date on what God is doing in and through you. One suggestion might be for your team to set up a blog for your trip and to assign one person to be responsible for updating that site. The site can be used from the beginning to inform people of the status of the team and give them specific needs to remember in prayer. It can also be the connection for everyone's supporters and family to stay in touch with the team while they are on the field. Keep in mind that, in some areas, internet access may not be available.

THE CULTURAL ADAPTATION PROCESS

The host will be the key for your success within the country where you are serving. Not only will they be able to assist you with the ministry side of things, but they will also be able to smooth the way for you culturally. They will be the source of wisdom if you have questions about cultural appropriateness. Please follow their lead and ask before you act!

In every culture there are certain activities that may be off-limits for your team or for the believers that you have come to serve. Some limits may be due to government regulations, denominational restrictions or just culturally acceptable social guidelines.

For most travelers, there is a cultural transition process. It may be helpful for you to think about this process in four phases:

- *The Romantic or Tourist Phase*: Everything is interesting and exciting. There is a feeling of euphoria. Cultural differences are easily blurred or overlooked.

- *The "You've Lost that Loving Feeling" Phase*: Curiosity gives way to frustration; feelings of irritation, anger, loneliness and helplessness combine with fatigue resulting in classic culture shock.

- *The Recovery Phase*: New ideas and practices don't seem as strange, self-confidence returns, negative feelings subside.

- *The Acceptance Phase*: Differences are understood and even expected, humor returns, able to feel relaxed.

You may easily move from one phase to the next during a brief time and be totally at ease with a new culture; however, should you find yourself "stuck" in a less-than-comfortable phase, there is hope for change. Your circumstances may not change but your heart can change toward the people and circumstances.

Ask the Lord to help you to see the people as He does—with loving eyes. You will be amazed at what He will do in and through you. You are a guest in their culture so be a student of their culture in order that you might be a servant in their culture.

AFTER
THE TRIP

What should you expect when you return?

Many things will happen during your ministry trip. There will be friendships formed with believers, young and old, who will touch your heart with their simple and deep faith. There will be wonderful memories made that will never be captured by a mere photo. There will be lessons learned that you didn't even know you needed to learn. You will never be the same. All too soon, the time will come for you to pack your bags and make the long journey home.

DEBRIEF

Debrief verbally with your team. Just before you head for home, while still on location, it will be important for the team to meet to debrief. Your team leader will want to spend time hearing your ideas about the time together. This is a great time to share stories and testimonies and praise the Lord as a team for what He accomplished.

Complete a written evaluation form. Also, before you leave the field of ministry, your team leader will ask each team member to complete a written evaluation of the trip. This information is used to monitor the positive and negative elements of the trip so that your church or ministry can continue to make improvements that will be beneficial to future teams from the United States and workers in partnering ministries. Your honesty and clarity will be a big help to future ministry.

There is a sample evaluation form located in the Appendix

section of this book.

REPORT

The journey home may be tiring and you will probably anticipate all the responsibilities waiting for you, but your ministry is not over. Resist the urge to move too quickly to a "finally I'm home" mindset.

Remember your sending team. Your financial supporters and prayer partners will be anxiously waiting to hear from you so perhaps you could use your time on the flight home to think through what you will share and how you can best convey your experience to them. Whether you write a letter, send an email, make a personal visit or have opportunity to share in a church service, these important partners need to hear from you.

Prepare what you will say. You may have 2, 5 or even 10 minutes or you may be asked to share for an hour, but you will be asked, "How was your trip?" Be prepared, you may have opportunity sooner than you imagine. When reporting on your trip, keep these principles in mind:

- *Be specific.* Rather than making comments like, "The people were nice, "or "It was fun," tell about a special memory or event. That will make it more meaningful.

- *Be selective.* You can't share everything. Choose a couple of highlights of how God used you to minister to another or spoke to you while you were away. Try not to overwhelm them with all of your pictures. Show 3-4 of you doing ministry rather than sightseeing.

- *Be positive.* Instead of telling stories of illnesses and problems, encourage them by relating the more positive results of your trip. Let them get excited with you about God's amazing love and power.

- **Be respectful.** Avoid any descriptions of your ministry experience that might seem disrespectful of the people you served or the culture you experienced. Tell about your team members' strengths rather than their embarrassing moments.

- **Be humble.** Remember that you were part of a team; a team that stayed, prayed and gave and a team that now continues the work that was started.

- **Be grateful.** The people that prayed and gave to your work should know by your words and actions that you appreciate the part they played in your ministry.

ACTION

You're home. The suitcase is unpacked and the laundry is done. You've sent thank you notes to all your financial supporters and prayer partners. You shared with your family all the details of this amazing adventure and you participated in a team report to your church family. Now you are done. Or are you?

Don't lose the learning. At home or abroad God calls us to be his ambassadors. God allowed you to experience missions from a new perspective. What will you do with this special gift? Do you really want it to end? Or do you want to let it change you long term? You grew spiritually, so how are you going to keep that spiritual growth moving in a positive direction? Your vision for the lost grew, so how are you going to be more involved in reaching the lost? You saw God use you, so how are you going to let God use you in a new way in your hometown, home church, in your family, in your own neighborhood, at work, etc. You saw ministry up close and first hand, so how can you be involved in the future?

Complete a personal growth interview. Every team member should undergo personal growth as a result of their mission trip so each individual should participate in a personal growth interview with their team leader after the trip is over. The goal for this time is to capture and capitalize on that growth. Based on that assessment each individual will develop an action plan for ongoing life change.

There is a sample Action Plan form in the Appendix section of this book.

Plan for the future. Perhaps God will call you to return to your new "home away from home" on another ministry trip. Or He might ask you to give financially to a ministry you worked with in order to help your new brothers and sisters in Christ. Maybe God would have you start a prayer group to pray for the ministry specifically on a regular basis. Or maybe He will call you to go again. It could be that this time it will be to a new place or maybe even for a longer time.

It is our prayer that the time you served will create in you a stronger desire to seek Him, listen carefully to His voice and lovingly obey His call. We look forward to helping you in your quest to follow God's leading in your life. God bless you!

GENERAL
RECOMMENDATIONS

Answers to Your Questions

There are, invariably, questions that arise in each unique ministry situation. These guidelines will begin to answer some of the questions you will have and will help to avoid any unnecessary uncertainty.

Commitment

A short-term mission trip is a serious commitment. The activities related to the actual trip are only one part of that commitment. In addition, team members are asked to dedicate adequate time to their training, the completion and timely submission of an individual application and other forms, the preparation required for their particular trip, completing necessary reports and evaluations, participating in team debriefings and creating a personal action plan upon returning home.

Team Member Qualifications

Christian ministries seek to represent God well and to serve the Church around the world faithfully. They endeavor to maintain high standards in all they do including the mission trips they lead. We recognize that God gives each one of His children special gifts and uses each individual in a unique way.

Each application for short-term ministry should be considered on the basis of the applicant's own merits as reflected in his or her application and references.

Personal and Spiritual Qualifications

- A genuine heartfelt love for Jesus

- A desire to serve God and others

- An understanding of the basic doctrines of the Christian faith

- A recognizable level of spiritual maturity

- A love for people and a desire to see them come to know Jesus as Savior and Lord of their lives and to mature in their faith

- A degree of experience in the area in which they are planning to serve

- A sensitivity to a different culture and a willingness to adapt to such

- The blessing and support of the applicant's home church

Educational Qualifications

- Educational qualifications will depend upon the type of short-term service in which the applicant wishes to be involved in. This will be evaluated on a case-by-case basis.

There is a Code of Conduct in the Appendix section of this book which will help each team member to understand the expectations for their behavior while serving.

Cultural Awareness and Sensitivity

Since your purpose is to further God's Kingdom, it is expected that team members will put all their effort into reaching this purpose by serving our brothers and sisters in Christ diligently and carefully.

Due to various cultural and legal restrictions your team leader will give you clear guidelines concerning your activities within the partnering country. Your cooperation will either be a help or a hindrance to future ministry so please be wise and follow the advice given by your global partner.

When working in a cross-cultural setting, flexibility and understanding are paramount to effective ministry. Every effort will be made to coordinate and plan ministry activities well ahead of time, but we ask you to be flexible in the event of unplanned changes in the program. Remember that the goal is to serve our brothers and sisters in Christ and minister to their needs. Flexibility is the key.

Passports

A valid passport is necessary for mission trip participants (including minors). Detailed information about obtaining passports for minors is available at the U.S. Department of State's website. Passport applications are available from your post office and normally take four to six weeks to process. Be sure to plan ahead for this in case of any delay.

Make sure that your passport will be valid at least six months following your final day of travel. Passports that expire within six months of the end of travel may not be valid for travel in certain countries. It is wise to make several copies of your passport prior to your trip. We suggest you leave a copy at home, carry one with you in a separate compartment from the original and give one to the team leader for safe keeping.

Traveling with Minors

Some mission trips are tailor-made for families and others are great opportunities for teens. Whenever minors are included (even if traveling with parents), they should be included in the trip preparations, be assigned to meaningful ministry assignments while away and be given opportunity for growth when they return home. If we are including minors in the team, we should serve them in the same ways we serve adult team members. Even young children can be impacted spiritually by a mission trip and they can certainly be used of God to impact others along the way. Recognizing their value to your team will help you to make good decisions about their involvement as well as their care.

Incidents of child abductions, disputed custody cases and child trafficking are on the rise. Therefore, the U.S. Customs and Border Protection (CBP) strongly recommends that unless the child is accompanied by **both** parents, the parent or other adult traveling with the child should carry with them a letter giving permission to travel with the child. The letter should state that the parent acknowledges that this individual has permission to travel out of the country with their child. It should also include the "who, what, where, when, why of the trip along with contact information for the parents not traveling with the minor. In cases where neither parent is traveling with the child, **both** parents should provide letters of permission. Easy-to-complete forms can be found online. Completed letters or forms should be notarized.

It's possible that this documentation will not be requested at the border. However, if they do ask, and you don't have it, you may be detained until the circumstances of the child traveling without both parents can be fully assessed. If there is no second parent with legal claims to the child (deceased, sole custody, etc.) any other relevant paperwork such as a court decision, birth certificate naming only one parent, death certificate, etc. would be useful to have on hand.

Adults traveling with children should also be aware that, while the U.S. does not require this documentation, many other countries do; failure to produce notarized permission letters and/or birth certificates could result in travelers being refused entry or exit at international borders.

Medical and General Release Forms

Each team member should complete a General Release and a Medical Release form as part of the application process. These can be kept on file at your church or ministry office. Medical forms are confidential. However, copies should be given to the team leader in case of emergencies while away.

Health Insurance

Each team member should have health insurance while traveling. Check with your insurance company to ensure your coverage extends outside of the United States. Proof of health insurance coverage should be submitted with applications. A copy of the policy section verifying coverage or a statement from the insurance agent stating that you are covered overseas is sufficient as proof of coverage. Those who do not have health insurance that extends outside the U.S. can purchase temporary travel health insurance. Some countries will only recognize a national health insurance and in those cases this will be purchased upon arrival. Your team leader will let you know if this will be necessary and this expense can be included in your trip budget.

Travel Insurance

In addition to coverage for medical needs, temporary travel insurance policies are available and it is usually wise to purchase this insurance. These policies have coverage for lost luggage, lost tickets, etc. for a minimal cost. To help prepare for the unexpected, travel insurance can be included in the trip budget.

Luggage

Due to changing airline regulations, it is always best to check with the carrier for luggage guidelines (weight and dimensions) ahead of time. Some of the smaller, international carriers have tighter restrictions so be aware of this when packing. Careful observation of these requirements will keep your team from being unduly delayed. Individual team members may be responsible for any fees incurred for oversize, overweight or too many pieces of luggage.

It is extremely important that team members bring no more luggage than they can *comfortably* carry themselves! In some cases luggage must be carried over fairly long distances. This is important to keep in mind when you're packing for the trip. Transportation to and from the airport and to the ministry site is very often by bus and/or train. These are often crowded and will not wait for you. You must be able to handle your own luggage as everyone else will have their own luggage to manage.

In addition to any ministry supplies, clothing and personal items, feel free to bring such things as books, travel guides, musical instruments, travel games, etc. Use discernment in bringing expensive electronic devices (IPods, game systems, cameras, etc.) as they have sometimes been proven to be counterproductive to effective ministry. Bear in mind the example that you are setting for the believers you are serving. You will be watched closely by them. Remember that the focus is on ministry to others.

Various countries require immunizations and you may be required to show a certificate upon arrival. Your team leader will alert you to the needs accordingly. We recommend that you get a tetanus booster if you have not had one in the past five years.

Traveling may cause stomach problems or digestion issues due to a change in water and eating habits. With this in mind you may want to bring over-the-counter drugs that you are familiar with.

If you have a problem with flying or driving, be sure to carry motion sickness pills with you. Familiar brands of medicine and vitamins are not always available. If you regularly take prescription medications, be sure to pack enough for your trip. Medications should be carried in your carry-on luggage according to airline guidelines.

Team Budgets and Finances

The trip budget is usually based on details and activities provided by your host. The first draft of the budget is usually established many months in advance of the trip. This first-draft budget should be reviewed 30-60 days before the departure date. On rare occasions, trip budgets must be adjusted after they are finalized.

Adjustments to the budget are made as appropriate, if:
- Dates are changed before the tickets are purchased
- Ticket prices change before purchase
- Additional expenses are anticipated by the national ministry in relationship to the ministry project

- Number of participating team members changes
- Exchange rate changes dramatically

Ministry expenses may be shared by the team and should be noted in the individual budgets. Your team leader will purchase all tickets, vouchers and coupons needed for your ministry trip and will work with the host to make all necessary arrangements for your transportation and accommodations.

Funds designated for mission trips can be given to your church or ministry and are receipted as such. Funds given in excess of the trip budget are usually used to further the ministry.

Financial Support

Individuals participating in mission trips may make a donation to cover the expenses for their trip. These funds can usually be receipted as a tax deductible gift if desired.

Participants may also seek financial support from their churches and/or individuals. Those who desire to support individuals in this program may send donations to the applicable office. Checks should be made payable to your church or ministry and clearly designated for your support as a short-term missionary. In this way, a tax deductible receipt can be issued to the donor and your account will reflect the donation. Team members will receive regular reports concerning their account status. Gifts can also usually be given online. Check with your church or ministry for details.

In certain cases, a church or individual may wish to provide you with money for your personal expenses (spending money, souvenirs, etc.). These funds do not need to be reported. In these cases, a receipt cannot be issued.

Personal Money

The trip budget includes housing and food, transportation involved with ministry, visas and vouchers—all the things necessary for the ministry project. Team members should be responsible to provide for their own personal expenses while traveling to and from the ministry destination and for personal spending on location. This would include sightseeing excursions, snacks, souvenirs, phone calls, visits to internet cafes, etc.

Take every precaution to safeguard your cash as you travel. Keep it in a safe place and avoid displaying large amounts of cash in crowded areas. Credit cards and traveler's checks are not always accepted when travelling overseas. Occasionally banks will even refuse to exchange an otherwise legitimate bill simply because of a mark on the face of the bill or the series date so ask for new bills at your bank before travelling if at all possible.

Cancellation

On rare occasions, team members may find that they need to cancel their participation. In this situation, the individual support account funds raised for a trip can be relinquished to cover the expenses incurred on behalf of the individual and to support the remaining team members.

Special Gifts

If the team or sending church wishes to send a special gift for the global partners, whether it is for the planned ministry project or another, it is best for those funds to be sent to the applicable office where they will be processed and disbursed to the appropriate account. Gifts given directly to the ministry partners cannot be receipted properly.

Carrying Ministry Cash

Transferring large sums of money through electronic means is difficult and unwise in some countries. It may be necessary in such cases for the team to carry cash for the trip expenses. At times team members may be asked to take on the responsibility of carrying part of the funds needed for the ministry portion of the trip. This should only done if absolutely necessary and a team member has the option to decline. Team members willing to assist can be provided with additional training in order to follow cash handling procedures.

A Caution Concerning Promises

It is important that you be careful about raising the expectations of the people you are working with during the ministry trip. Off-hand comments such as "maybe we can" or "would you like to" may be misunderstood as promises. While these kinds of statements do not necessarily indicate a commitment in our culture, they do in others. Avoid making suggestions about sending them things once you have returned to home or about any other things that you do not really intend to do anything about. If you are approached by a national about a specific financial or other need, ALWAYS suggest to the individual that they talk to your team leader about that need. Don't ever promise to take the information back to your home church or other contacts in the U.S. without being asked to do so by your team leader.

APPENDIX

Sample Team Assignments

Release of Rights

Code of Conduct

Financial Accountability Form

Support Discovery Resources

Potential Ministry Partners Worksheet

Preparing a Personal Testimony

List of Additional Resources

Bible Studies for Pre-Trip Preparation

Daily Team Devotionals from Nehemiah

Getting Ready to Head Home

Team Member Evaluation Form

Action Plan

Sample Team Assignments

These assignments are designed for the entire team to share the responsibilities for the ministry trip and are flexible. Each assignment could be the responsibility of one person or more than one, for smaller teams someone may be assigned more than one. Please adapt the following assignments to meet the needs of your team.

Team Leader:
Responsibilities include: Scheduling meetings for the team before departure, training the team, collecting all paperwork, arranging transport for the team members and overseeing that travel documents are properly completed at each port of entry. The team leader will work closely with the host for scheduling and is to shepherd the team to oversee their success on the field.

Journalist:
Responsibilities include: Documenting the team's experiences in the field including faith-building and spiritual events with geographical locations, times of day, weather conditions, living conditions, possible background information on people, numbers involved in events, activities of team members, etc. The journalist will work closely with the photographer/ videographer and prayer-praise teams to coordinate email information for correspondence with the support team.

Photographer/ Videographer:
Responsibilities include: Recording imagery that would be the most accurate view of the team's experiences in preparation and on the field. Team photos are important, but the interaction of the team with the people we are serving is essential. Photos

and videos will be used to communicate to the 'Home Team' the needs of the people and to feel like they are there with the team so they will work with the journalist and prayer-praise teams to piece together detailed emails for the support team.

Prayer-Praise Coordinator:
Responsibilities include: Documenting both prayers and praises for the team members during team meetings and praying with the team members individually as well as corporately. The prayer-praise coordinator will work with the journalist and photographer/ videographer on email communications with the support team enabling them to pray for the team before and during the trip so they can experience God's provision for the team. The prayer-praise coordinator will also work with the worship leader for times of worship/devotion/prayer.

Accountant:
Responsibilities include: Maintaining and dispensing the team finances. Keeping detailed reports of expenditures (invoice/receipts) relating to hotel accommodations, traveling expenses (buses, cabs, etc.), meals, etc. The accountant will be required to complete an expense report and submit all financial documents to the applicable office typically within two weeks of the teams return to the US. The accountant will work with team leader.

Luggage Coordinator:
Responsibilities include: Tagging and tracking all checked luggage. Keeping a log is recommended. Check with all airlines prior to departure to learn their guidelines for luggage as they may vary. Oversee the delivery of luggage to the appropriate person. The luggage coordinator will work with the team leader.

Medic:
Responsibilities include: Carrying a first-aid kit while the team is on the field. Handle any minor medical issues that may occur. Be

aware of any pre-existing medical conditions for which a member is taking medication. Retain a file of medical emergency information forms for all team members. Check with team members frequently on their physical status. Notify the team leader of any problems.

Worship Team:
Responsibilities include: Assisting the team in entering the presence of the Lord through music, prayer and Bible study. Work closely with prayer-praise coordinator.

Host Appreciation Coordinator:
Responsibilities include: Working with the team leader to discover interests and needs of the host and/or host family and international partners in order to select a gift and card of appreciation from the team.

Special Projects Coordinator:
Responsibilities include: Preparing materials and supplies for special projects such as face painting, teaching English or performing dramas. Works closely with team leader.

Release of Rights

We live in a world full of rights. Jesus Christ, God the Son, laid down His rights to become a man, to serve, and to sacrifice His life (Phil. 2:5-11 and Mark 10:45). We ask that you consider laying down some of your rights for the sake of others during this trip. We ask that you entrust your rights to the Lord and leave the results to Him. Take time to search your heart and willingness to surrender these rights to the Lord (Romans 12:1). Put a check mark next to each statement as you come to that place with the Lord.

I GIVE UP MY RIGHT TO:

√ A comfortable bed

√ Having three meals a day

√ Having familiar food

√ Dressing fashionably

√ Seeing results

√ Control of myself

√ Control of others

√ Control of circumstances

√ Making decisions

√ Taking up offense

√ Being successful

√ Being understood

√ Being heard

√ Being right

√ Having pleasant experiences

I ENTRUST TO GOD:

✓ His purposes and timing   ✓ My health and strength

✓ My preferences of food   ✓ My acceptance in Him

✓ My strength and endurance   ✓ My reputation

✓ His workmanship in others   ✓ My security in His love

✓ My need for recognition   ✓ My deepest needs

✓ My need for the Holy Spirit control

✓ His desire to make me Christ-like

✓ The privilege of suffering for Him

✓ His sovereign hand on my life

✓ My need for His righteousness

I give God permission to do anything He desires to me, with me, in me, and through me in order that I might glorify Him.

Marelyn Williams   5-22-23
Signature   Date

56

Code of Conduct

As a team member, you are expected to conduct yourself according to the highest standards of integrity and morality. Agreeing to serve on a team means that you are agreeing to adhere and abide by all provided guidelines, policies, and procedures. Your commitment to this code of conduct means you say, "I will…" to the following:

- Attend **all** team meetings prior to departure and during the trip.

- Go as a servant-disciple of Jesus Christ. This attitude will be reflected in dealing with my fellow team members and leader(s), the missionaries and nationals I meet during the trip.

- Accept and submit to the leadership and authority of the team leader(s) and promise to abide by his or her decisions regarding this mission trip.

- Respect the advice given concerning attire, eating and drinking, and other such traditions that will help to assimilate our team on the field.

- Guard my tongue. I will not make derogatory comments or get involved in arguments regarding people, politics, sports, religion, race, or traditions. I will refrain from meddling, complaining and using obscene or insensitive humor.

- Refrain from using tobacco, alcoholic beverages, or illegal drugs at any time during the mission trip.

- Abstain from dating for the duration of the trip. I will not seek romantic relationships with a team member, team leader, overseas worker or nationals I may meet on my trip.

- Consult first with the team leader or host before I promise or give a gift, so I don't create problems for my host or others after the team returns home.

- Refrain from any other behavior or activity that would hinder my ministry or the ministry of my team.

I have read and understand and agree to the above standards for conduct. I understand that if my conduct is considered unsatisfactory, an endangerment to the success of the trip and mediation fails to correct my behavior that my participation will end and I will return home immediately at my own expense.

Marilyn Williams 5-22-23

Signature   Date

Financial Accountability Form

Each member of a team is responsible to cover their expenses for the trip. Your team leader will provide support for each individual to assist in reaching the financial goals individually and for the team. Since fundraising is unique and challenging, both to the one raising support and to the donor, the timing of the gifts is not always predictable. There will be set guidelines and deadlines in order to facilitate travel plans. Each team member will be responsible to refer to the trip schedule in order to know when funds are due. The church or ministry will process and issue receipts for all donations received for the trip.

Team Member Commitment

Following the first meeting I must decide if I am willing and called to participate. If I consider that this is God's desire for me to move forward I will submit a non-refundable deposit of $_____ no later than ___/___/___ which will be applied to my personal trip account.

I will do everything I can according to the established guidelines to raise the necessary funds to cover my expenses for the trip in relation to the predetermined schedule.

In the event that I am unable to raise my portion of expenses according to the due dates given me by my team leader, I have two options:

- I can withdraw my name from the team roster. Any purchases made on my behalf for team trip expenses will be charged to my trip account and I understand that I am personally responsible for any non-refundable expenses up to the date I withdraw my name from the team roster.

- I can personally pay the balance due in order to continue with trip plans. If additional support is received towards my account within 30 days after completion of the trip, those gifts will be credited to my account and, if a credit exists, I may be reimbursed for my expenses at that time.

If, for any reason, I am unable to participate in this trip, I will be financially responsible for any non-refundable expenses associated with the purchase of airline tickets, hotel reservations, travel insurance, etc.

Any funds that are raised over and above the team goal will be considered an unrestricted donation and will be used to further the ministry around the world. Financial gifts designated for a specific trip, team or team member's short-term ministry trip expenses are not refunded, transferred, or held for future trips.

Name _____

Trip Name _____

Trip Dates _____

I understand and agree to the above.

_____   _____
Signature   Date

Support Discovery Resources

One of the most important things you can do as a team member is to invite others to be involved in the ministry, by prayer or through their financial support. Today there are many ways to communicate with others. Telephones, cell phones, instant messaging, text messaging, and social media sites are all used to communicate our ideas. In spite of these modern advances in communication people still like to receive letters. A personal letter communicates the value of the relationship because of the time and effort invested in the act of writing.

You will want to express the value that you place in the relationship with your support partners. It is good to keep them informed at each step in your progress. The following is a simple plan that you can follow.

Letter #1

Your first letter will be one of introduction. You will want to be brief and to the point so that potential partners will want to read the whole thing. It is important that they understand that this is more than just a request for money, but an opportunity to be involved with you in this short-term ministry project. You might include:

- o Who you are
- o Who is the organization you are going with
- o What you will be doing on this trip
- o When and how long you will be traveling
- o Why the ministry is significant
- o How they can help
- o A response card

In your communication to your donors you will also want to include instructions for giving online if available.

Letter #2 (Optional)

This letter will be sent prior to your departure. It will let those on your mailing list know how God is already at work and how they can continue to support you and the project. You might include:

- o What you are working on
- o What your current needs are
- o Specific requests and answers to prayer
- o A response card

Letter #3 (Optional)

Unless you plan ahead this will probably be the last thing you think of while you are on the field, until it is too late. Your partners need to be kept informed and will enjoy a postcard from you while you are on the field. Purchase postcards early on and write a few each day. If the team has been able to create a blog site for people to visit that is great and you will want to let your partners know how to access the site, but it does not replace a personal note.

Letter #4

Once you have returned home you will want to send a final letter to report on the trip. Your partners will be anxious to hear from you and learn what God has done. You might include:

- o One or two highlights from your trip
- o Pictures of you in ministry
- o How you sensed God using you
- o How their partnership made a difference in your trip
- o Thank them for joining you on this trip

By following this plan, you will effectively communicate with the people that God has led to be a part of your ministry and this mission. They will feel an integral part of what happened. They will be able to rejoice with you at the amazing things God did in and through you as a result of this trip.

SAMPLE LETTER

Dear Friends,

"Blessed be the Lord God Almighty, who was and is, and is to come." How exciting it is to watch the Lord work on both a global and personal level. It has been a privilege for Amy to serve at XYZ Church in the children's ministry department and I have seen God using me in my role as the new principal at North High School.

God has recently placed a unique opportunity for us to respond to a huge need in Romanian churches. Through a mission organization that is partnering with XYZ Church, we have been asked to participate in a church camp for children and a leadership summit at a local church in Romania.

Amy and I will travel to Romania for two weeks in June, where we will be serving side by side with a Romania team of Christian leaders. The team from the U.S. will be providing some Basic English classes for the children in order to create interest in the Romanian parents who desire this for their children. The Romanian team will be presenting the truth of God's Word each day. Together we pray that this week would benefit the children in the local church. Our team will also be working closely with the Romanian team to provide encouragement and support. The team is also scheduled to provide leadership workshops with local churches in the village where the camp is located. Amy and I are honored to be included in this unique opportunity and look forward to our time with the Romanian Christians.

As we prayed about our trip, God placed the names of a few friends that have been a blessing to us as we have grown. We love each of you and thank God for your presence in our lives. We are asking that you pray for us as we travel and teach and to consider a special gift to help cover travel expenses, materials and supplies for the Romanian leaders we will serve on this trip. Our total estimated cost is $4,500.00. If you would like to join us by praying or contributing we would ask you to have you complete the enclosed response card. You will receive a tax-deductible receipt for gifts that are sent for this trip.

May God bless you for your support of Amy and I and this important work with a mission organization in Romania.

In Christ,

George and Amy

SAMPLE LETTER

Dear friends and family,

It is with great excitement that I am writing today. God has recently placed a unique opportunity for me to partner with churches in Uganda. In November 2015, I will be traveling to Kisoro, Uganda to help a mission organization conduct a leadership training program for those already serving in Christian ministry.

This mission organization is an international, interdenominational Christian organization with the goal of coming alongside ministry leaders to equip, encourage and inspire them to follow God's call as they take the Word of God to the people they serve. This particular course will be focusing on team building and preparing to meet the needs of the children in churches.

I am asking you to pray for me while I travel abroad and serve and to consider a one-time gift to help cover travel expenses, materials and supplies for the camp. The total cost of this trip is $2,875. If you feel the Lord is leading you to give, please send your check with my name written in the memo line. Your donation will be used to cover my trip expenses. Any excess funds will be used towards the trip and/or released to the mission organization's general fund. If you would like to be a part of our "home team" through giving, praying or donating miles, please fill out the form provided and mail to the mission organization using the enclosed envelope.

To give online, simply log on to www.xyzorganization.org. Press the "Donate" button on any website page. You will be taken to a PayPal site where you can enter your payment information. Before your payment is completed, you will have the option of adding instructions. Put my name in the instructions box and your gift will be designated for my support. If you have any questions please email the mission organization at admin@xyzorganization.org.

It is a blessing to be able to join God in the work that He is doing around the world and to share it with you. Each of you is an indescribable blessing to me and I thank God for your presence in my life.

In Christ,

(Signature)

SAMPLE RESPONSE CARD

Uganda – January 2015

Name of Team Member _____

Your Name _____

Your Email Address _____

Your Phone Number _____

Check any that apply

- o   Yes! I want to be on your email list and receive updates during your trip.
- o   Yes! I want to be on your prayer team. I commit to pray for you and your team every day you are traveling.
- o   Yes! I want to be a part of your financial support team.

Please make your check payable to _____. Please write my name in the memo portion of the check. Please use the enclosed envelope to mail this form and your check directly to _____. If I should raise more funds than I need for my trip expenses, the excess funds will go towards our team expenses and/or released to the general fund.

Potential Ministry Partners Worksheet

Carefully and prayerfully consider the relationships you have. Think of those you know through your church and community groups. Include family members and friends or even co-workers. God will direct you to those He wants to be included.

Keeping track of those who are joining you in ministry is critical. This will allow you an opportunity to keep in contact prior to your departure, possibly during the trip and most definitely once you return home. This form is a sample for you to use or adapt. The style of the form is not important. What does matter is that you have and use the information.

Use this list to pray for these people as well as for a mailing list.

Name	Contact Info	Prayer	Donor	Thanks

Preparing a Personal Testimony

GIVING YOUR TESTIMONY DURING THE TRIP

There may be times before, during and after you participate in a mission trip when you will be invited to share your faith story with a large group, with co-workers over dinner or perhaps just one-on-one. Each team member should be prepared.

Step 1

Pray for insight on what God would like you to share. You may not feel your testimony is very thrilling, but be encouraged that it is exciting to become a Christian, no matter how it happened.

Step 2

Think through the three parts of your testimony.

    a. The first part is before you became a Christian. How your life was before knowing Christ. What were the desires of your heart? Where did you feel empty? How did you attempt to fill those empty spots in your life?

    b. The second part is to share how you came to know Christ. How did it happen? What was the situation? Did you attend a church service or special event? Was it the result of someone else's life? What scripture did God use to show you your need? This is a brief presentation of the message of salvation.

    c. The third part is to tell how your life has changed as a result. In what ways did your life change? How are your choices different? What is God teaching you at this point in your life? Try to tie this into the "before" parts to show the difference Jesus has made in your life.

Step 3

Once you have thought through the three steps take time to write out your testimony. Try to connect the three points with a central idea. Then practice it out loud, possibly in front of a mirror. Finally, tell your story to another Christian friend and ask for input.

- Keep things brief. Assume that five minutes is your maximum allowable time. It can be lengthened easier than shortened.

- Be honest without giving focus to the sinful lifestyle before Jesus.

- Use scripture where appropriate.

- Avoid using "Christianese." Assume that your listeners don't know anything about the message of salvation.

- Emphasize what God did for you, not what you did. Avoid giving the impression that the Christian life is without problems.

- Try not to seem preachy. Just tell them your story.

GIVING YOUR TESTIMONY AFTER THE TRIP

When you return from your trip you will want to prepare a different type of testimony to share with your prayer partners, donors, friends and family. You may be asked to share with your home church or Bible study group in a large group setting or perhaps on a more intimate level over coffee, but these ministry partners *will* want to hear from you. They will all have many questions about your trip and you will want to be prepared to answer them clearly, concisely and with confidence. It will be another opportunity for you to be used of God.

Step 1

Again, begin with prayer. This ministry opportunity was uniquely created for you by God. You may have travelled with a group of 5 or 25, but your individual experience will change you. That is what people will want to hear about.

Step 2

Plan what you will say.

a. Recap for your listeners how you came to the point of going on this mission trip. Why were you drawn to this particular trip? What did you anticipate before you left home? What did you think you would be facing and learning?

b. Communicate what made the trip memorable. What did you do while you were there? How and when did you sense God using you to effectively minister to others? Is there one experience or individual that stands out from the rest? Was there a passage of scripture that He used to encourage you or challenge you?

c. Convey to your audience how the trip impacted your life. What lesson did God teach you while you were away? How will this trip change your future? How has this changed your view of mission trips or of the world?

d. Remind them that this trip was God's work made possible with their help. Thank them for their involvement in the work that God did, is now doing and will continue to do because of the efforts on this trip.

<u>Step 3</u>

Think it through. Write it out. Practice it. Gather a few pictures or souvenirs to show.

- Be prepared to share for 5, 10 or maybe even 30 minutes depending on the circumstances.

- Be personal and honest. Your supporters will want to know what it was like for you!

Be positive about the team, the nationals and the ministry as a whole. There will not be time to tell everything and some stories need not be shared so be selective in the ones you do choose to tell. Consider how it will be received by the listeners.

Additional Resources

Books

Team-Building Activities for Every Group
 By Alanna Jones

A Guide to Short-term Missions
 By H. Leon Greene, MD

Operational World 21ˢᵗ Century Edition

Culture to Culture-Mission Trips Do's and Don'ts
 By Nan Leaptrott

Websites

Cultural and country information

www.operationworld.org
www.odci.gov/cia/publications/pub.html
www.expateexchange.com
http://david.snu.ed/hcubbet/yeshua.htm
http://www.sherisentsi.com

Travel tips

http://travel.state.gov/travel/tips/tips

Bible Studies for Pre-Trip Preparation

Bible Study 1

Bible passage to read: John 15:1-17

1. In this passage, Jesus chose a very common object to display a unique series of relationships.

   - *Who is Jesus speaking to in this passage?*

     disciples, us

   - *How does Jesus describe himself?*

     true vine

   - *How does he portray his Father?*

     the gardner

2. Think about those you are going to serve on this trip.

   - *Why do you think our national partners are eager to have our team come?*

     many hands help get the product out the door

- *How does someone become part of "the vine"?*

  believe in Jesus

- *What would you share with a child that wanted to believe in Jesus?*

  Jesus is your friend, if you hold onto him he will hold onto you.

3. Now think about yourself.

- *What is your relationship to "the vine?"*

  Good but could be better. I rely on Him but sometimes put Him off/back burner.

- *What must you do to remain "in the vine?"*

  read my Bible and seek out His words for me.

- *What is the result of "remaining in the vine?"*

  will become a disciple of God

Bible Study 2

Bible passage to read: John 15:1-4

1. Jesus compares God the Father to a gardener.

   - *What does a gardener need to do in order to keep the branches producing fruit?*

     prune (take off) the dead and dying ones. The ones not producing

   - *How does God, the Master Gardener, "prune" us?*

     daily trials

   - *Why does he "prune" us?*

     to make us more like him to bring us closer to him

2. During this trip we will experience many new things, interact with people of different cultures, work and live in close quarters.

   - *What type of "pruning" might be done on this trip?*

     being tolerant of others who don't "work" like we do

   - *What should be our response to the "pruning" of God?*

     thank you and use it to grow

77

Bible Study 3

Bible passage to read: John 15:1-4

1. In order for the branches to continue to be healthy and productive they must remain connected to the vine.

   - *What can you and I do to stay connected to Jesus?*

     Study the Bible

   - *How do you practice this in real life?*

     apply what I learn from His teachings

   - *What is the "fruit" that is produced when we remain connected to Jesus?*

     other Christians

2. Staying connected to our spiritual source of strength will be critical for a productive time of ministry on our trip.

   - *What are some steps we can take as a group to ensure we are able to bear fruit?*

     morning study fellowship

- *What can we anticipate will be the results?*

lengty .

Bible Study 4

Bible passage to read: John 15:5-8

1. Jesus is the vine. We are the branches. We are to remain in him in order to bear fruit.

   - *As a reminder, what does it mean to remain in Jesus?*

   - *How much can we accomplish apart from Jesus? What happens to the branches that are no longer attached to the vine?*

   - *In what ways do we try to accomplish work apart from Jesus? How can we avoid trying to do our work on this trip apart from Jesus?*

2. The terminology changes in this passage from the previous verses.

   - *How does the terminology change from verse 4?*

- *What are we able to do if we remain in Jesus?*

- *What are the results of remaining in Jesus? What can we confidently ask God to produce as a result of our ministry trip?*

Bible Study 5

Bible passage to read: John 15:9-14

1. The Father loved the Son. The Son loves his followers.

   - *What was Jesus' response to the Father's love? What are some examples of Christ's obedience to the Father?*

   - *How are the disciples to respond to the love of Christ? Is this always easy? Why or why not?*

2. In verse 12, Jesus gives a clear command to his followers.

   - *What is the command? Why is that sometimes a difficult command to obey?*

   - *What are the results of obeying this command?*

- *How might obeying this command impact us? How would it impact those we are serving alongside during this trip? What difference might it make to those we are ministering to during this time?*

Bible Study 6

Bible passage to read: John 15:9-17

1. In verses 14 and 15, Jesus makes a profound
    statement regarding his relationship to his followers.

    *   *What is the statement? What reasons does Jesus
        give for the change?*

    *   *What do you think is the significance of this
        change?*

    *   *How does this affect how you view your
        relationship with Jesus?*

2. Jesus makes it clear to his followers in verse 16 that
    he is responsible for the selection of those who will
    serve him.

    *   *When you think about Jesus choosing you how do
        you feel?*

- *What does he say we were chosen to do?*

- *What kind of fruit are we to produce?*

3. This passage ends with a promise and a command.

   - *What is the promise? What is the command?*

   - *Where else in God's Word do we see this promise and command? What should be our response to these?*

Daily Team Devotionals
from Nehemiah

Session 1

Bible passage to read: Nehemiah 1:1-11

1. Nehemiah's daily job was that he was cupbearer to the king. He wasn't a full-time Christian worker and he wasn't necessarily prepared for the task set before him. He was just an ordinary person.

    • *As you think through the Bible, what other ordinary people can you think of that were greatly used of God?*

    • *How does God use ordinary people today?*

    • *Why do you think God enjoys using ordinary people so much?*

2. Nehemiah was a cupbearer who was called into wall-building. It was definitely not in his comfort zone.

    • *How do you feel about doing something that you may not be used to doing on this short-term ministry trip?*

    • *How do you think the skills Nehemiah developed as a cupbearer might be transferable to the task of wall-building?*

    • *What skills has God developed through your experience that may be of use to Him on this trip?*

3. Nehemiah was deeply touched when he heard about the needs of the people of Jerusalem. He even wept upon hearing the news of their plight.

    • *How has God touched your heart as you have learned of the needs of the people you will be working with on the ministry field?*

4. When Nehemiah heard the news of the broken-down wall, he remembered the reason it had been broken. It was because of God's judgment on the people of Israel because of their disobedience. He then mourned, fasted and prayed in preparation for the work God was already moving in his heart to do.

   - *What do you perceive to be the spiritual needs of the people with whom you will be working on your mission trip?*

   - *What do you need to do to be spiritually ready for the short-term ministry God is calling you to do?*

Session 2

Bible passage to read: Nehemiah 1:11 - 2:9

1. Nehemiah knew he would need to have the king's favor if he was to get help from the king. He knew he could not do it on his own, but needed the help of others.

   - *How has it felt to ask others to participate with you as you embark on this missionary journey?*

   - *What importance do you think God places on that part of the preparation for a mission trip (getting others involved)?*

2. The king never left his home, but was an integral part in the ministry that was accomplished.

   - *How is God using those who never leave their homes, but are an integral part what you are doing on the field?*

   - *How can you help them to feel that their part is important?*

3. Nehemiah planned for his journey and was concerned about safety. It's natural and normal to want to be safe. Cross-cultural experiences don't always feel "safe," though.

    • *What have you learned so far about your own safety on the mission trip?*

Session 3

Bible passage to read: Nehemiah 2:11-20

1. Nehemiah didn't share with everyone initially about what God was asking him to do.

    • *What do you think the reasons were for Nehemiah's need for privacy?*

    • *Has God ever shown you something that was so precious it couldn't be shared with others right away?*

2. Nehemiah wanted to evaluate the needs "up-close and personal" so he examined the broken down walls carefully.

    • *How has your sense of the needs of the mission field changed now that you have seen it in-person?*

3. Nehemiah boldly stated the need to the people and challenged them to take ownership of the project.

    • *Who has God used to challenge you to be involved in mission?*

4. As soon as everyone agreed to work together, the opposition started. In verse 20, Nehemiah states clearly that God will be the one to give success.

    • *What have you seen so far on your trip that could ONLY be God's hand at work, helping your team succeed?*

Session 4

Bible passage to read: Nehemiah 3:1-32

1. Chapter 3 of the book of Nehemiah is a list of all the people that worked together in the wall building process.

   • *Why do you think it is important to God that these names are listed in this book?*

   • *In addition to the "official" team members, who would be on your list of "People God Used" on this mission trip?*

2. The work described in chapter 3 is very difficult, physically taxing manual labor.

   • *What has been especially physically challenging for you on this mission trip?*

   • *How has God strengthened you for the task at hand?*

3. In verse 5, it speaks of those who would not put their shoulder to the work under their supervisors.

   • *Why is it important for team members to follow leaders on mission trips?*

   • *How has your "supervisor" (your team leader) been a blessing to you on this trip?*

4. In verse 12, it states that Shallum was helped by his daughters.

   • *What advantages can you see to having both male and female team members?*

5. The passage talks about different groups of priests working alongside lay people.

   • *What benefits do you see to having people in vocational Christian service work alongside in ministry with those who are dedicated Christians but with secular jobs?*

Session 5

Bible passage to read: Nehemiah 4:1-23

Questions for discussion:

1. In verse 1-3, Sanballat and Tobiah are quoted as they ridicule the wall-building work of the Jews. They imply that the work is impossible for the people to do and that the work will not last.

    * *What impossible tasks has God allowed your team to accomplish on this trip?*

    * *How have you stayed encouraged when you thought that the work was too much to do?*

    * *What part of the work God has asked you to do on this trip will last forever? What will pass away?*

2. Verse 6 says the people worked with all their heart.

    * *Who on your team have you seen work in this way and how have you known they were putting their whole heart into it?*

3. Nehemiah and his team of laborers met the opposition by praying and by standing watch.

    • *How can we as a team apply the principle of "standing watch" in our ministry context?*

    • *How do you plan to honor, inform and thank those who prayed diligently for you while you were on this trip?*

4. In verse 19 and 20, Nehemiah reminds the team to stick closely together and to gather together to defend themselves against attack.

    • *How has God encouraged you as you have followed the same pattern on your team?*

Session 6

Bible passage to read: Nehemiah 6:1-14

1. Sanballat, Tobiah and Geshem were great enemies of the work God was doing through His people.

   • *What enemies have we encountered on this mission trip?*

2. Several techniques were used to discourage the workers: distraction ("come to Ono"), persistence ("four times they sent the message"), gossip ("an unsealed letter"), accusations ("it is reported"), lies ("you are just making it up") and temptation ("so that I would commit a sin").

   • *What techniques has the enemy used to discourage you in your task on this trip?*

   • *Why do you think the enemy works so hard to discourage us in this task?*

Session 7

Bible passage to read: Nehemiah 6:15, 16; 8:2-12

Questions for discussion:

1. The wall was completed in an amazing 52 days!

    • *What amazing things has God accomplished through your team during this trip?*

2. The "closing ceremonies" after the wall was completed included a reading from the Word of God. When the people heard it, they bowed with faces to the ground and worshiped God. They wept over their sin, forgetting for a moment to celebrate the work God did through them.

    • *As you have experienced God using you on this trip, how has He made you more aware of the need to follow Him closely?*

3. Nehemiah encouraged the people to celebrate God's work through them and to have a party with food and drinks, remembering how God had been their strength.

    • *Why was it important to pause to celebrate rather than going on with business as usual?*

    • *How can your team follow this same pattern when you return to your home?*

4. The last phrase recorded in the book of Nehemiah is, "Remember me with favor, O my God."

    • *Each of us will have memories of this trip, but what is memorable in God's eyes, do you think?*

Getting Ready to Head Home

You have just been through a time that will forever change you. Whether the time went by without any complications or was filled with challenges, YOU are different. You will look at things from a new perspective and others will notice.

Gather together as a group before you leave and have a time to share what God did in your lives. Here are some questions to get you started.

- What did you come prepared to do?

- Did you feel prepared? If not, what would have helped to make you feel better prepared?

- If you could change one thing about this trip, what would you change?

- How did God change your life while you were on this trip?

The people who supported you through their financial gifts and or their prayers are as much a part of this ministry as you are. They will want to hear your stories. To not tell your story is to keep the blessing to yourself. You will want to plan and prepare what you will say.

- What will you tell people?

- What methods will you use to tell your story?

- If you can only tell one story, what will it be?

Team Member Evaluation Questions

You will be provided with an evaluation form to fill out and submit to your team leader. It may be helpful for you to know in advance the questions on that form. These forms help to ensure that the ministry is profitable for everyone. Your input is vital.

They are as follows:

1. How would you rate your overall short-term ministry experience? Please rate it on a scale of 1-10: _____
    Explain:

2. Based on your experience, would you participate in a short-term mission trip again? Why or why not?

3. During the trip, what went especially well? What were the highlights for you?

4. Did you feel adequately prepared for your time of ministry?
    Explain:

5. Were the materials and help that you received adequate for your time of ministry?
    Explain:

6. Do you have suggestions regarding the preparation of future teams?

7. Please share any positive or negative comments or suggestions that you have for future trips.

8. Did you take any photographs, slides or video footage that you would be willing to share with us for use in our publications? If yes, what is the best way for us to get those from you?

9. Please share with us your stories of how God worked in your life during your short-term ministry experience (what you experienced, how God used you, what He did in you, etc.) Please include any memorable events and/or quotable quotes.

Action Plan

An action plan is significant to your personal development. It will be a time of reflection and response to God. When it comes time to develop an action plan be sure to consider your full experience from your trip.

What were the key moments for you during your preparation and during your time of ministry?

What did you find yourself struggling with during this time?

How did you experience God using you in the lives of your teammates and in the lives of those you went to serve?

What do you sense God is telling you about yourself? About those you served?

Based on what you've heard from God about yourself, what specific personal development goals can you set in response to Him?

Based on what you've heard from God, what are specific ministry goals you can set for yourself in response to Him? Consider how He is asking you to make a long-term difference in the ministry field you experienced.

What steps will you need to take in the next 3 months to accomplish that goal? In 6 months? Beyond?

Next 3 months

Next 6 months

Beyond

Mission Trip Journal

_____

_____

_____

_____

_____

_____

_____

_____

_____

_____

_____

_____

_____

_____

_____

_____

_____

What is ENDURING TREASURE MINISTRIES?

ETM DISTINCTIVES

- **Eternal Focus** – We believe in focusing on what lasts for eternity – God's Word and people. We believe that a life dedicated to bringing the eternal principles of God's Word to the people He dearly loves is a life well-spent.

- **Loving Leadership** – We believe that love is God's central message and, therefore, must be the motivation for all of life and ministry. Ministry that is motivated by love will include speaking the truth in love, acting in love and leading from love.

- **Practical Biblical Strategies** – We believe that the Bible is practical and that living according to it works. Everyone is looking for practical strategies to meet life and ministry challenges and these can readily be found in God's Word.

- **Transparency** – We believe that a commitment to transparency glorifies God and results in ministry credibility. Therefore, we will remain steadfast in our pledge to transparency in all of our relationships. This includes our guarantee to remain above reproach in all of our financial dealings.

- **Global Perspective** - We believe that God's Word was given to the whole world and we desire to help our brothers and sisters in Christ around the world with practical tools for life and ministry.

ETM STRATEGY

Enduring Treasure for Christian Leaders – We have a passion to come alongside and provide fuel for ministry leaders based on the principles God's Word. We offer on-site ministry consultation, dynamic training courses, interactive online communities and individualized coaching. We seek to encourage, strengthen and equip ministry leaders to continue to follow God's calling as they take the Word of God to the people that He has placed in their lives.

Enduring Treasure for Life – God created each individual with a unique purpose but life often crowds out that truth and can blur the vision that God has given. Enduring Treasure's certified Life Coaches are here with a listening ear to celebrate individual uniqueness, provide reassuring support, and offer loving counsel from a biblical and practical perspective.

Enduring Treasure Publishing – Provides discipleship tools and practical ministry resources that make the principles found in God's written Word accessible to His servants. Current projects include both printed materials and online resources designed to meet the needs of our local and international ministry partners.

Enduring Treasure Global Adventures – The Global Adventures program of Enduring Treasure provides opportunities for God's people to become directly involved in cross-cultural experiences working together with and supporting those already serving throughout various regions. Through meaningful short-term ventures, participants share in the work of the ministry and are able to experience lasting personal growth and maintain long-term relationships with those in the field.

Enduring Treasure for Global Outreach – Right now, God's servants are busy doing ministry on every continent of the world. Some of these have vast resources and experience abundant harvest. Others meet indifference to their message, face overwhelming obstacles and are ministering under extreme conditions. Enduring Treasure is passionate about the people in need of God's truth all around the world and especially in East/Central Africa where needs are so acute. We're committed to supporting our international partners in ways which will have lasting impact.

FREQUENTLY ASKED QUESTIONS ABOUT ETM

What does ETM do?
Enduring Treasure Ministries seeks to aid Christian leaders through on-site and online training, individual biblical life coaching and practical leadership tools for use in sharing God's Word. Our passion is to see ministry leaders throughout the world encouraged and strengthened to do the work that God has called them to do.

What churches and denominations does ETM assist?
Enduring Treasure Ministries is an interdenominational ministry. We are involved with and are supported by churches and individuals from a variety of denominational backgrounds.

Does ETM have a Board of Directors?
Yes, godly men and women who are in agreement with ETM's vision and are committed to its purposes meet regularly to give counsel and provide oversight for the work. We are blessed to

have amazing Christian people providing visionary leadership for the organization.

How is ETM supported?
ETM is primarily supported by the donations of those God has asked to participate in the ministry financially. Income is also generated through resources, training, and coaching.

Are financial gifts to ETM used wisely?
ETM strictly adheres to principles of excellence in stewardship. ETM operates under the governing authority of an active board of directors. Financial reports are open to the public upon request.

Made in the USA
Monee, IL
03 April 2023

31214269R00075